Guided Reading and Study

Sound and Light

PRENTICE HALL Science Explorer

Boston, Massachusetts
Upper Saddle River, New Jersey

ISBN 0-13-190184-2   7 8 9 10   09 08 07

Sound and Light

Science Explorer ▪ *Target Reading Skills Handbook*

⟳ Target Reading Skills

Identifying Main Ideas

Identifying the main idea helps you understand what you are reading. Sometimes the main idea can be easy to find. For example, suppose that you are reading just one paragraph. Very often you will find the main idea in the first sentence, the topic sentence. The other sentences in the paragraph provide supporting details or support the ideas in the topic sentence.

Sometimes, however, the first sentence is not the topic sentence. Sometimes you may have to look further. In those cases, it might help to read the paragraph and summarize what you have read. Your summary can give you the main idea.

A textbook has many paragraphs, each one with its own main idea. However, just as a paragraph has a main idea and supporting details, so does the text under each heading in your textbook. Sometimes the main idea is the heading itself. Other times it is more difficult to find. You may have to infer a main idea by combining information from several paragraphs.

To practice this skill, you can use a graphic organizer that looks like this one.

Main Idea		
Detail	**Detail**	**Detail**
a.	b.	c.

Outlining

Outlining shows you how supporting details relate to main ideas. You can make an outline as you read. Using this skill can make you a more careful reader.

Your outline can be made up of sentences, simple phrases, or single words. What matters is that you follow a formal structure. To outline while you read, use a plan like this one.

I. Section Title
  A. Main Heading
    1. Subheading
      a. Detail
      b. Detail
      c. Detail

The main ideas or topics are labeled as Roman numerals. The supporting details or subtopics are labeled A, B, C, and so on. Other levels of supporting information can be added under heads. When you outline in this way, you are deciding just how important a piece of information is.

Science Explorer ▪ *Target Reading Skills Handbook*

Comparing and Contrasting

You can use comparing and contrasting to better understand similarities and differences between two or more concepts. Look for clue words as you read. When concepts or topics are similar, you will probably see words such as *also, just as, like, likewise,* or *in the same way.* When concepts or topics are different, you will see *but, however, although, whereas, on the other hand,* or *unlike.*

To use this skill, it sometimes helps to make a Venn diagram. In this type of graphic organizer, the similarities are in the middle, where the two circles overlap.

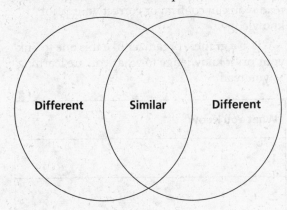

Relating Cause and Effect

Identifying causes and effects can help you understand the relationships among events. A cause is what makes something happen. An effect is what happens. In science, many actions cause other actions to occur.

Sometimes you have to look hard to see a cause-and-effect relationship in reading. You can watch for clue words to help you identify causes and effects. Look for *because, so, since, therefore, results, cause,* or *lead to.*

Sometimes a cause-and-effect relationship occurs in a chain. For example, an effect can have more than one cause, or a cause can have several effects. Seeing and understanding the relationships helps you understand science processes. You can use a graphic organizer like this one.

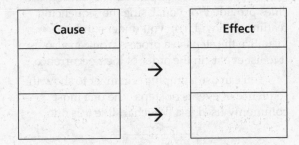

Asking Questions

Your textbook is organized using headings and subheadings. You can read the material under those headings by turning each heading into a question. For example, you might change the heading "Protecting Yourself During an Earthquake" to "How can you protect yourself during an earthquake?" Asking questions in this way will help you look for answers while reading. You can use a graphic organizer like this one to ask questions.

Question	Answer

Science Explorer ▪ *Target Reading Skills Handbook*

Sequencing

Sequencing is the order in which a series of events occurs. As you read, look for clue words that tell you the sequence or the order in which things happen. You see words such as *first, next, then,* or *finally.* When a process is being described, watch for numbered steps. Sometimes there are clues provided for you. Using the sequencing reading skill will help you understand and visualize the steps in a process. You can also use it to list events in the order of their occurrence.

You can use a graphic organizer to show the sequence of events or steps. The one most commonly used is a flowchart like this one.

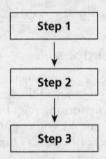

Sometimes, though, a cycle diagram works better.

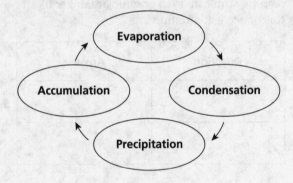

Using Prior Knowledge

Use prior knowledge to relate what you are reading to something that you already know. It is easier to learn when you can link new ideas to something that is already familiar to you. For example, if you know that fish are actually breathing oxygen that is dissolved in water, you wil be able to understand how or why gills work.

Using prior knowledge can help you make logical assumptions or draw conclusions about what you are reading. But be careful. Your prior knowledge might sometimes be wrong. As you read, you can confirm or correct your prior knowledge.

Use a graphic organizer like this one to link your prior knowledge to what you are learning as you read.

What You Know
1.
2.
3.

What You Learned
1.
2.
3.

Science Explorer ▪ *Target Reading Skills Handbook*

Previewing Visuals

Looking at visuals before you read can help you better understand a topic. Preview the visuals by reading labels and captions. For example, if you preview the visuals in a chapter about volcanoes, you will see more than just photographs of erupting volcanoes. You will see maps, diagrams, and photographs of rocks. These might tell you that you will learn where volcanoes are found, how they form, and what sort of rock is created when volcanoes erupt. Previewing visuals helps you understand and enjoy what you read.

One way to apply this strategy is to choose a few photographs, diagrams, or other visuals to preview. Then write questions about what you see. Answer the questions as you read.

Identifying Supporting Evidence

In science, you will read about hypotheses. A hypothesis is a possible explanation for scientific observations made by scientists or an answer to a scientific question. A hypothesis is tested over and over again. The tests may produce evidence that supports the hypothesis. When enough supporting evidence is collected, a hypothesis may become a theory.

Identifying supporting evidence in your reading can help you understand a hypothesis or theory. Evidence is made up of facts. Facts are information that can be confirmed by testing or observation.

When you are identifying supporting evidence, a graphic organizer like this one can be helpful.

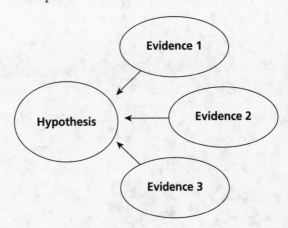

Building Vocabulary

To understand what someone is saying, you have to know the language that person is speaking. To understand science, you need to know what the words mean.

There are many ways to build your vocabulary. You can look up the meaning of a new word in a dictionary or glossary. Then you can write its definition in your own words. You can use the new word in a sentence. To figure out the meaning of a new word, you can use context clues or surrounding words. Look for prefixes and suffixes in the new word to help you break it down. Building vocabulary will get easier with practice.

Characteristics of Waves ▪ *Guided Reading and Study*

What Are Waves? (pp. 6–10)

This section explains what causes waves and identifies two types of waves.

Use Target Reading Skills

Before you read the passage for each heading, fill in the top box with what you know.
After you have read the passage, fill in the bottom box with what you have learned.

What You Know
I. Waves are high and low.
2.
3.
4.
5.

What You Learned
I.
2.
3.
4.
5.

Waves and Energy (pp. 7–8)

1. What is a wave?

_____

_____

2. The material through which a wave travels is called a(n)

_____.

3. Circle the letter of each of the following that can act as mediums.
   a. solids
   b. liquids
   c. gases
   d. empty space

Characteristics of Waves · *Guided Reading and Study*

What Are Waves? *(continued)*

4. Waves that require a medium through which to travel are called _____.

5. Is the following sentence true or false? When waves travel through a medium, they carry the medium with them. _____

6. Explain what happens to the motion of a duck on the surface of a pond when a wave passes under it.

   _____

   _____

   _____

   _____

7. Give an example of a wave that can travel through empty space.

   _____

   _____

8. Mechanical waves are produced when a source of energy causes a medium to _____.

9. What is a vibration?

   _____

   _____

   _____

Types of Waves (pp. 8–10)

10. How are mechanical waves classified?

    _____

    _____

11. Waves that move the medium at right angles to the direction in which the waves are traveling are called _____.

12. Suppose you move the free end of a rope up and down to create a wave. In that case, the rope is the medium. What is the relationship between the movement of the wave and the movement of the particles of the medium?

    _____

    _____

    _____

    _____

Characteristics of Waves · *Guided Reading and Study*

13. The highest parts of a transverse wave are called

_____.

14. The lowest parts of a transverse wave are called

_____.

15. What type of waves move the particles of the medium parallel to the direction in which the waves are traveling?

_____

16. In longitudinal waves in a spring, the parts where the coils are close together are called _____.

17. In longitudinal waves in a spring, the parts where the coils are spread out are called _____.

18. Complete this concept map about types of waves.

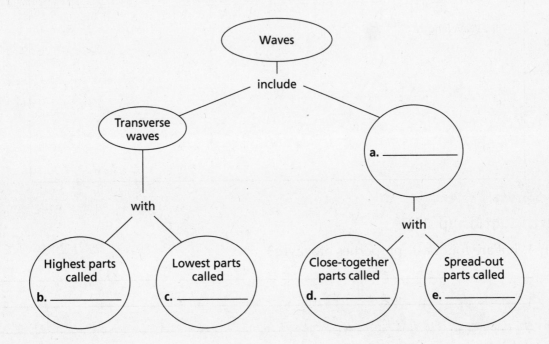

19. If you were to draw a longitudinal wave, you should think of the compressions as _____ on a transverse wave and the rarefactions as _____ on a transverse wave..

Characteristics of Waves · *Guided Reading and Study*

Properties of Waves (pp. 11–15)

This section describes the basic properties of waves. It also explains how a wave's speed is related to its wavelength and frequency.

Use Target Reading Skills

As you read about the properties of waves, make an outline using the red headings for the main ideas and the blue headings for the supporting ideas.

Properties of waves
I. Amplitude
A. Amplitude of Transverse Waves
B.
II. Wavelength
III.

Introduction (p. 11)

1. What are four basic properties of waves?

   _____

   _____

   _____

Amplitude (p. 12)

2. The maximum distance the particles of the medium carrying a wave move away from their rest position is called the wave's

   _____.

3. Explain what the amplitude of a water wave is.

   _____

   _____

   _____

Characteristics of Waves · *Guided Reading and Study*

4. The amplitude of a wave is a direct measure of its

   _____.

5. What is the amplitude of a longitudinal wave?

   _____

   _____

   _____

   _____

6. Circle the letter of each phrase that correctly defines the amplitude of a transverse wave.

   a. The distance from the bottom of a trough to the top of a crest
   b. The maximum distance the particles of the medium move up or down from their rest position
   c. The maximum distance from one point on the rest position to another point on the rest position
   d. The distance from the rest position to a crest or to a trough

7. Suppose a longitudinal wave has crowded compressions and loose rarefactions. Does it have a large or a small amplitude?

   _____

Wavelength (p. 13)

8. The distance between two corresponding parts of a wave is its

   _____.

9. How can you find the wavelength of a transverse wave?

   _____

   _____

   _____

10. How can you find the wavelength of a longitudinal wave?

    _____

    _____

    _____

    _____

Characteristics of Waves • *Guided Reading and Study*

Properties of Waves (continued)

Frequency (p. 13)

11. The number of complete waves that pass a given point in a certain amount of time is called the wave's _____.

12. If you make a wave in a rope so that one wave passes every second, what is its frequency?

_____

13. Circle the letter of the unit used to measure frequency.

    a. watt

    b. seconds

    c. joule

    d. hertz

Speed (pp. 14–15)

14. The speed of a wave is how far the wave travels in one unit of

_____.

Complete the following formulas.

15. Speed = _____

16. Frequency = _____

17. Wavelength = _____

18. Circle the letter of each sentence that is true about the speed of waves.

    a. Speed increases as a wavelength increases.

    b. In a given medium and under the same conditions, the speed of a wave is constant.

    c. If the temperature and pressure of air change, the speed of sound waves traveling through the air will change.

    d. The same wave may travel at different speeds in different mediums.

19. If you increase the frequency of a wave, the wavelength must

_____.

Characteristics of Waves • *Guided Reading and Study*

Interactions of Waves (pp. 17–23)

This section describes how waves bounce back, bend and interact with each other.

Use Target Reading Skills

Before reading the section, write questions based on the red headings and record them in the graphic organizer below. As you read, write the answers to your questions in the graphic organizer.

Interactions of waves

Question	Answer
How are waves reflected?	Waves are reflected . . .

Reflection (p. 18)

1. On the illustration below, write labels and draw arrows to show the location of the angle of incidence and the angle of reflection.

2. The bouncing back of a wave when it hits a surface through which it cannot pass is called _____.

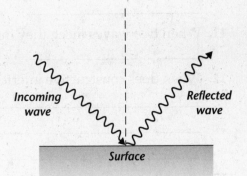

Incoming wave   Reflected wave   Surface

3. What does the law of reflection state?

_____

_____

4. Is the following sentence true or false? All waves obey the law of reflection.

_____

Characteristics of Waves · *Guided Reading and Study*

Interactions of Waves (continued)

Refraction (p. 19)

5. What happens when a wave moves from one medium into another medium at an angle?

   _____

   _____

   _____

6. The bending of waves as they enter a different medium is called

   _____.

7. All waves change speed when they enter a new medium, but they don't always bend. When does bending occur?

   _____

   _____

   _____

8. The bending of a wave entering a new medium occurs because the two sides of the wave are traveling at different _____.

Diffraction (p. 20)

9. What happens when a wave passes a barrier or moves through a hole in a barrier?

   _____

   _____

10. The bending of waves around the edge of a barrier is known as

    _____.

11. When two waves meet, they interact. This interaction is called

    _____.

12. When does constructive interference occur?

    _____

    _____

13. What happens when the crests of two waves overlap?

    _____

    _____

    _____

Characteristics of Waves • *Guided Reading and Study*

Interference (pp. 20–21)

14. When two waves interact to produce a wave of larger amplitude, the interaction is called _____.

15. In Figure 10, why does the wave labeled 2 on the right have an amplitude of zero?

_____

_____

_____

_____

16. What happens when destructive interference occurs between waves with different amplitudes?

_____

_____

_____

_____

Match the type of wave interaction with its description.

Interaction	Description
____ 17. refraction	a. Two waves combine to make a wave with a smaller amplitude.
____ 18. diffraction	b. A wave bends as it moves from one medium to another.
____ 19. constructive interference	c. Two waves combine to make a wave with a larger amplitude.
____ 20. destructive interference	d. A wave bounces back from a surface.
____ 21. reflection	e. Waves bend and spread out as they pass around an obstacle or through an opening in a barrier.

Characteristics of Waves · *Guided Reading and Study*

Interactions of Waves (continued)

Standing Waves (pp. 22–23)

22. What is a standing wave?

_____

_____

_____

_____

_____

23. A point of zero amplitude on a standing wave is called a(n)
_____.

24. The points of maximum amplitude on a standing wave are called
_____.

25. Is the following sentence true or false? Most objects have a natural
frequency of vibration. _____

26. When does resonance occur?

_____

_____

_____

_____

Name _____ Date _____ Class _____

Seismic Waves (pp. 26–29)

This section explains how earthquakes produce waves that move through Earth.

Use Target Reading Skills

As you read the section, note the definition of each key term. Also note other details in the paragraph that contains the definition. Then use all the information to write a sentence using the key term.

a. seismic wave

_____

_____

b. P wave

_____

_____

c. S wave

_____

_____

d. surface wave

_____

_____

e. tsunami

_____

_____

f. seismograph

_____

_____

Types of Seismic Waves (pp. 27–28)

1. What happens when stress in rock builds up inside Earth?

_____

_____

_____

2. The waves produced by earthquakes are known as

_____.

Characteristics of Waves · *Guided Reading and Study*

Seismic Waves (continued)

3. Circle the letter of each sentence that is true about seismic waves.
    a. Some seismic waves are longitudinal.
    b. Seismic waves do not carry energy.
    c. There is only one type of seismic wave.
    d. Seismic waves ripple out in all directions from the point where the earthquake occurred.

4. Why can't S waves travel through Earth's core?

    _____

    _____

5. Which type of seismic waves arrives at distant points before any other seismic waves? _____

6. Which type of seismic waves produces the most severe ground movements? _____

7. Which type of seismic waves cannot be detected on the side of Earth opposite an earthquake? _____

8. What are tsunamis?

    _____

    _____

9. Complete the table about seismic waves.

Seismic Waves		
Type of Seismic Wave	**Transverse or Longitudinal?**	**Travel Characteristics**
a.	b.	Travel through all parts of Earth
S waves	c.	Travel through Earth but not through d. _____
e.	f.	Travel only along Earth's g. _____

Detecting Seismic Waves (p. 29)

10. Circle the letter of the instrument scientists use to detect earthquakes.
    a. rarefactions
    b. telegraphs
    c. seismographs
    d. tsunamis

Characteristics of Waves · *Guided Reading and Study*

11. What does a seismograph record?

_____

12. What is the frame of a seismograph attached to?

_____

_____

13. What happens to a seismograph's frame when seismic waves arrive?

_____

14. How can scientists tell how far away an earthquake was from a seismograph?

_____

_____

_____

15. How can scientists tell where an earthquake occurred?

_____

_____

16. Complete the flowchart about how geologists locate valuable substances under Earth's surface.

To find out what is underground, geologists set off **a.** _____.

↓

The explosives produce **b.** _____.

↓

The seismic waves reflect from structures deep **c.** _____.

↓

The reflected seismic waves are recorded by **d.** _____ located around the site of the explosion.

Characteristics of Waves ▪ *Key Terms*

Key Terms

The block of letters below contains 16 key terms from the chapter. You might find them across, down, or on the diagonal. Use the clues to identify the terms you need to find. Circle each of the terms in the block of letters.

Clues

1. A disturbance that transfers energy from place to place

2. The ability to do work

3. The material through which a wave travels

4. A repeated back-and-forth or up-and-down motion

5. The highest part of a transverse wave

6. The lowest part of a transverse wave

7. The maximum distance the particles of the medium carrying the wave move away from their rest position

8. The distance between two corresponding parts of a wave

9. The number of complete waves that pass a given point in a certain amount of time

10. The unit in which wave frequency is measured

11. The bending of waves due to a change of speed as waves enter a new medium at an angle

12. The bending and spreading out of waves around the edge of a barrier and spreading out

13. A point of zero amplitude on a standing wave

14. A point of maximum amplitude on a standing wave

15. What occurs when external vibrations match an object's natural frequency

16. A huge surface wave on the ocean caused by an underwater earthquake

d	t	s	u	n	a	m	i	p	a	q	w
i	v	i	b	r	a	t	i	o	n	m	a
f	r	e	q	u	e	n	c	y	t	a	v
f	u	n	n	p	w	b	v	x	i	m	e
r	e	f	r	a	c	t	i	o	n	p	l
a	x	e	n	e	r	g	y	u	o	l	e
c	i	w	a	v	e	z	a	p	d	i	n
t	z	e	e	v	s	z	u	j	e	t	g
i	o	d	d	e	t	x	w	e	g	u	t
o	o	u	t	r	o	u	g	h	y	d	h
n	i	r	e	s	o	n	a	n	c	e	r
n	y	h	m	e	d	i	u	m	r	t	z

Sound · *Guided Reading and Study*

The Nature of Sound (pp. 36–41)

This section explains what sound is how sound waves interact, and it identifies factors that affect the speed of sound.

Use Target Reading Skills

As you read the Interactions of Sound Waves *section, write the main idea in a graphic organizer like the one below. Then write three supporting details that further explain the main idea.*

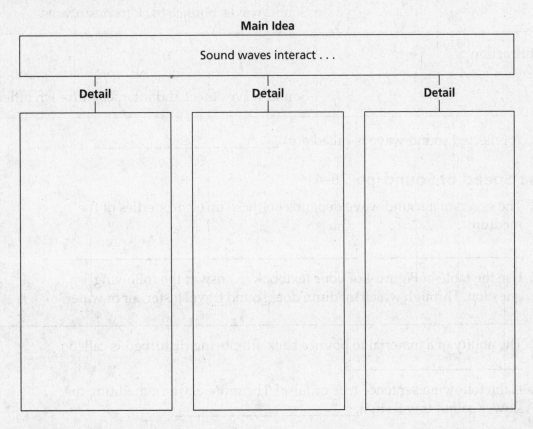

Main Idea

Sound waves interact . . .

Detail   **Detail**   **Detail**

Sound Waves (pp. 36–37)

1. What is sound?

   _____

   _____

2. A sound wave begins with a _____.

3. Is the following sentence true or false? Sound waves can travel without a medium. _____

Sound • *Guided Reading and Study*

The Nature of Sound (continued)

Interactions of Sound Waves (pp. 38–39)

4. Fill in the blanks in the table below.

Sound Wave Interactions

Type of Interaction	Description
a.	Sound waves bounce back from surfaces.
Diffraction	b.
c.	Sound waves meet and interact with each other.

5. A reflected sound wave is called a(n) _____.

The Speed of Sound (pp. 39–41)

6. The speed of a sound wave depends on these three properties of the medium.

_____   _____   _____

7. Use the table in Figure 4 of your textbook to answer the following question. Through which medium does sound travel faster, air or water?

_____

8. The ability of a material to bounce back after being disturbed is called _____.

9. Is the following sentence true or false? The more elastic a medium, the slower sound travels in it. _____

10. The amount of matter there is in a given amount of space is called _____.

11. Is the following sentence true or false? In materials in the same state of matter, sound travels more slowly in denser mediums. _____

12. Does sound travel more slowly through a given medium with a low temperature or high temperature?

_____

_____

_____

Sound · *Guided Reading and Study*

13. What is the speed of sound in air when the air has a temperature of 20°C?

_____

14. Why does sound travel more slowly at higher altitudes?

_____

_____

_____

15. In 1947, what did Captain Chuck Yeager do that nobody had ever done before?

_____

_____

_____

_____

16. Why is it easier to fly faster than the speed of sound at a high altitude?

_____

_____

_____

_____

Sound · *Guided Reading and Study*

Properties of Sound (pp. 42–47)

This section describes several properties of sound, including loudness and pitch. It also explains why pitch changes as the source of a sound moves.

Use Target Reading Skills

As you read the section, make an outline about the properties of sound. Use the red headings for the main ideas and the blue headings for the supporting ideas.

Properties of sound
I. Loudness
A. Energy of a sound source
B.
C.
II. Pitch
A.
B.
III.
A.
B.

Loudness (pp. 42–44)

1. What is loudness?

_____

_____

2. What two factors does loudness depend on?

_____

_____

_____

3. Is the following sentence true of false? The larger the amplitude of a sound wave, the louder the sound. _____

4. The amount of energy a sound wave carries per second through a unit area is called the wave's _____.

5. In what units is loudness measured?

_____

Sound · *Guided Reading and Study*

6. Why are loud sounds dangerous?

_____

_____

_____

Pitch (pp. 44–45)

7. What is the pitch of a sound?

_____

_____

_____

8. What does the pitch of a sound depend on?

_____

_____

9. Sound waves with frequencies above the normal human range of hearing are called _____.

10. Sound waves with frequencies below the normal human range of hearing are called _____.

11. Circle the letter of each sentence that is true about how a person changes the pitch of sounds when singing.

    a. A person relaxes the vocal cords to produce lower-frequency sound waves.

    b. A person stretches the vocal cords to produce lower-frequency sound waves.

    c. A person stretches the vocal cords to produce higher-frequency sound waves.

    d. A person relaxes the vocal cords to produce higher-frequency sound waves.

The Doppler Effect (pp. 46–47)

12. What is the Doppler effect?

_____

_____

_____

_____

13. The change in frequency of sound waves in the Doppler effect is heard as a change in _____.

Sound ▪ *Guided Reading and Study*

Properties of Sound *(continued)*

14. Why does the frequency of sound waves change for a listener when the sound source moves toward or away from the listener?

_____

_____

_____

_____

15. Complete the table about the Doppler effect.

Doppler Effect	
Action	**Change in Pitch — Higher or Lower?**
A police car with siren on moves toward you	a.
A train with a band playing moves away from you	b.
A train with a band playing moves toward you	c.
A police car with siren on moves away from you	d.

16. Is the following sentence true or false? A sonic boom is due to a shock wave that is produced when the sound barrier is broken.

_____

Sound · *Guided Reading and Study*

Music (pp. 48–52)

This section explains how different types of musical instruments produce and control sounds and why they have different sound qualities. The section also describes how acoustics is used in concert hall design.

Use Target Reading Skills

Preview Figure 15 in your textbook. Then write two questions that you have about the diagrams in the graphic organizer below. As you read, answer your questions.

Musical Instruments

Q. How is the pitch changed in each type of instrument?
A.
Q.
A.

Sound Quality (p. 49)

1. What is music?

   _____

   _____

2. The lowest natural frequency of an object is called the

   _____ .

3. How are overtones related to the fundamental tone?

   _____

   _____

4. Is the following sentence true or false? The sound quality of a musical instrument depends only on its fundamental tone and on resonance.

   _____

5. How does resonance affect the sound quality of a musical instrument?

   _____

   _____

   _____

Sound · *Guided Reading and Study*

Music (continued)

Groups of Musical Instruments (pp. 50–51)

6. How do musicians control the pitch of a musical instrument?

_____

_____

_____

7. How do musicians control the loudness of a musical instrument?

_____

_____

_____

8. What vibrates to produce sound on a brass instrument?

_____

_____

_____

9. What vibrates when a player blows into the mouthpiece of a woodwind instrument?

_____

_____

_____

10. Is the following sentence true of false? The pitch of a drum depends on its size, the material from which it is made, and the tension in the drumhead. _____

11. Complete the table by classifying each instrument into one of the major groups of instruments—Strings, Brass, Woodwinds, or Percussion.

Musical Instruments			
Instrument	**Major Group**	**Instrument**	**Major Group**
Guitar	a.	Cello	b.
Drums	c.	Tuba	d.
Violin	e.	Trumpet	f.
Cymbals	g.	Flute	h.
Clarinet	i.	Xylophone	j.

Sound • *Guided Reading and Study*

Acoustics (p. 52)

12. The study of how sounds interact with each other and the environment is called _____.

13. Circle the letter of the sentence that describes how destructive interference affects sound.

    a. It makes sounds louder.
    b. It increases the frequency of sound waves.
    c. It causes reverberation.
    d. It produces "dead spots" where loudness is reduced.

14. What is reverberation?

    _____

    _____

    _____

15. Why is acoustics used in the design of concert halls?

    _____

    _____

    _____

Name _____ Date _____ Class _____

How You Hear Sound (pp. 54–56)

This section describes how you hear sound and identifies causes of hearing loss.

Use Target Reading Skills

As you read The Human Ear, *make a flowchart that shows how you hear sound.*
Put the steps of the process in separate boxes in the order in which they occur.

How you hear sound

The outer ear funnels sound waves into the ear canal.

↓

Sound waves make the eardrum vibrate.

↓

↓

The Human Ear (pp. 54–55)

Match the three main sections of the ear with their functions.

Main Section

_____ 1. outer ear

_____ 2. middle ear

_____ 3. inner ear

Function

a. Transmits sound waves inward

b. Funnels sound waves

c. Transforms sound waves into a form that travels to the brain

4. The outermost part of your ear collects sound waves and directs them into a narrow region known as the _____.

5. What is the eardrum and where is it located?

6. What cavity of the inner ear is filled with fluid?

_____

Sound ▪ *Guided Reading and Study*

7. What part of the ear contains the three smallest bones in your body?

_____

Hearing Loss (p. 56)

8. Circle the letter of each choice that is a cause of hearing loss.
   a. aging
   b. injury
   c. nerve fibers
   d. infection

9. Why is it dangerous to put objects into your ear, even to clean it?

_____

_____

_____

_____

10. How can an infection cause hearing loss?

_____

_____

_____

11. What is the most common type of hearing loss?

_____

_____

_____

12. When you know you are going to be exposed to loud noises, what should you do to prevent hearing loss?

_____

_____

_____

13. Is the following sentence true or false? Hearing aids are amplifiers.

_____

Sound ▪ *Guided Reading and Study*

Using Sound (pp. 60–63)

This section explains how animals use ultrasound waves to navigate and find food and how people use ultrasound technologies such as sonar to observe things that cannot be seen directly.

Use Target Reading Skills

As you read, compare and contrast echolocation and sonar by completing the table below.

Using Sound

Feature	Echolocation	Sonar
Type of wave	Ultrasound	
Medium(s)		Water
Purposes		

Introduction (p. 60)

1. Is the following sentence true or false? Some animals communicate using sounds with frequencies that humans cannot hear.

   _____

Echolocation (p. 61)

2. The use of sound waves to determine distances or to locate objects is called _____.

3. What are two purposes for which bats and some other animals use echolocation?

   _____

   _____

4. Describe how a bat uses echolocation to avoid bumping into an object as it flies.

   _____

   _____

   _____

   _____

Sound · *Guided Reading and Study*

Ultrasound Technologies (pp. 62–63)

5. What is sonar?

_____

_____

_____

6. Circle the letter of each of the following choices that use of sonar.

   a. To raise sunken ships to the surface
   b. To determine water depth
   c. To map the ocean floor
   d. To find schools of fish

7. Complete the flowchart showing how sonar works to calculate the depth of the ocean.

> A sonar device sends **a.** _____ through the water.

↓

> When the sound waves hit the ocean floor, they bounce back, or **b.** _____ .

↓

> The reflected sound waves are detected by the **c.** _____ .

↓

> The sonar device measures the **d.** _____ it takes the reflected sound waves to return to the device.

Sound • *Guided Reading and Study*

Using Sound *(continued)*

8. Why do doctors use ultrasound imaging?

_____

_____

_____

9. What happens to ultrasound waves when they strike different parts of the body, such as bones and muscles?

_____

_____

_____

10. An ultrasound imaging device uses reflected ultrasound waves to create a picture called a _____.

11. Describe how a doctor uses ultrasound imaging to examine a developing baby before birth.

_____

_____

_____

_____

_____

_____

Key Terms

Use the clues to help you unscramble the key terms from the chapter. Then put the numbered letters in order to find the answer to the riddle.

Clues	Key Terms	
The membrane that separates the outer ear from the middle ear	mrrudae	__ __ __ __ __ __ __ 1
The cavity filled with fluid in the inner ear	ccleoah	__ __ __ __ __ __ __ 2
How high or low a sound seems to a person	hctip	__ __ __ __ __ 3
Sound waves with frequencies above the normal human range of hearing	dnuosartlu	__ __ __ __ __ __ __ __ __ __ 4
The ability of a material to bounce back after being disturbed	ttiiscyale	__ __ __ __ __ __ __ __ __ 5
System that uses reflected sound waves to detect and locate objects underwater	noars	__ __ __ __ __ 6
How well sounds can be heard in a particular room or hall	ccuossiat	__ __ __ __ __ __ __ __ __ 7
Your voice box	xyarnl	__ __ __ __ __ __ 8
A natural frequency of an object that is higher than the fundamental tone	vneeroot	__ __ __ __ __ __ __ __ 9
Sound with a pleasing quality	smcui	__ __ __ __ __ 10
A reflected sound wave	choe	__ __ __ __ 11
The amount of energy a sound wave carries per second through a unit area	ynittiens	__ __ __ __ __ __ __ __ __ 12

Riddle: What is the use of sound to find distance?

Answer:__ __ __ __ __ __ __ __ __ __ __ __
      1 2 3 4 5 6 7 8 9 10 11 12

The Electromagnetic Spectrum • *Guided Reading and Study*

The Nature of Electromagnetic Waves (pp. 70–73)

This section explains what an electromagnetic wave is and describes models of electromagnetic waves.

Use Target Reading Skills

As you read, make an outline about electromagnetic waves. Use the red headings for the main topics and the blue headings for the subtopics.

Nature of Electromagnetic Waves
I.   What is an Electromagnetic Wave?
A.   Producing Electromagnetic Waves
B.
C.
II.   Models of Electromagnetic Waves
A.
B.

What Is an Electromagnetic Wave? (pp. 71–72)

1. What are electromagnetic waves?

_____

_____

2. Is the following sentence true or false? Electromagnetic waves can transfer energy only through a medium. _____

3. What do electromagnetic waves consist of?

_____

_____

4. Complete the table about electric and magnetic fields.

Electric and Magnetic Fields	
Field	**Definition**
Electric field	A region in which
Magnetic field	A region in which

The Electromagnetic Spectrum ▪ *Guided Reading and Study*

5. The energy that is transferred by electromagnetic waves is called _____.

6. Circle the letter of each sentence that is true about electric and magnetic fields.

   a. An electromagnetic wave occurs when electric and magnetic fields vibrate at right angles to each other.
   b. A magnetic field is surrounded by an electric current.
   c. When an electric field vibrates, so does the magnetic field.
   d. Every charged particle is surrounded by a magnetic field.

7. Is the following sentence true or false? All electromagnetic waves travel at the same speed in a vacuum. _____

Models of Electromagnetic Waves (pp. 72–73)

8. Light has many of the properties of waves. But light can also act as though it is a stream of _____.

9. What happens when light passes through a polarizing filter?

   _____

   _____

10. The light that passes through a polarizing filter is called _____.

11. When light passes through a polarizing filter, does it have the properties of a wave or a particle?

   _____

12. Is the following sentence true or false? If two polarizing filters are placed so that one is rotated 90° from the other, all light can come through.

   _____

13. The movement of electrons in a substance when light is shined on it is called the _____.

14. The photoelectric effect can be explained by thinking of light as a stream of tiny packets of _____.

15. What are particles of light energy called? _____

The Electromagnetic Spectrum • *Guided Reading and Study*

Waves of the Electromagnetic Spectrum (pp. 74–81)

This section explains how electromagnetic waves differ from one another and how they are similar. It also describes the different waves of the electromagnetic spectrum.

Use Target Reading Skills

Before you read the section, preview Figure 3. Then write two questions that you have about the diagram in the graphic organizer below. As you read, answer your questions.

The Electromagnetic Spectrum

Q. Which electromagnetic waves have the shortest wavelength?	
A.	
Q.	
A.	

What Is the Electromagnetic Spectrum? (p. 75)

1. Circle the letter of each sentence that is true about electromagnetic waves.

   a. Different electromagnetic waves have different frequencies.
   b. All electromagnetic waves have the same wavelength.
   c. Different electromagnetic waves have different wavelengths.
   d. All electromagnetic waves travel at the same speed in a vacuum.

2. Circle the letter of each sentence that is true about electromagnetic waves.

   a. As the wavelength of electromagnetic waves decreases, the frequency increases.
   b. Waves with the longest wavelengths have the lowest frequencies.
   c. As the frequency of electromagnetic waves decreases, the wavelength increases.
   d. Waves with the shortest wavelengths have the lowest frequencies.

3. What is the name for the range of electromagnetic waves when they are placed in order of increasing frequency?

   _____

The Electromagnetic Spectrum ▪ *Guided Reading and Study*

4. Label the electromagnetic spectrum below with the names of the different waves that make up the spectrum.

Electromagnetic Spectrum

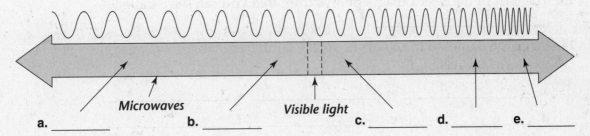

Microwaves   *Visible light*

a. _____   b. _____   c. _____   d. _____   e. _____

Radio Waves (p. 76)

5. Which type of electromagnetic waves carries television signals?

_____

6. What does a radio transform radio waves into?

_____

7. Is the following sentence true or false? Microwaves are the radio waves with the shortest wavelengths and highest frequencies.

_____

8. Is the following sentence true or false? Microwaves are used for cellular phone communication. _____

9. A system that uses reflected radio waves to detect objects and to measure their distance and speed is called _____.

Infrared Rays (p. 77)

10. The energy you feel as heat from an electric burner is carried by electromagnetic waves called _____.

11. Circle the letter of each sentence that is true about infrared rays.

   a. Infrared rays have a higher frequency than radio waves.
   b. Most objects give off some infrared rays.
   c. Infrared rays are sometimes called heat rays.
   d. Heat lamps give off no infrared rays.

12. A picture produced by an infrared camera using infrared rays is called a(n) _____.

The Electromagnetic Spectrum · *Guided Reading and Study*

Waves of the Electromagnetic Spectrum (continued)

Visible Light (p. 78)

13. The part of the electromagnetic spectrum that you can see is called

_____.

14. Write the names of the colors of visible light, from longest wavelength to shortest wavelength.

a. _____ b. _____ c. _____

d. _____ e. _____ f. _____

15. Is the following sentence true or false? White light is made up of a mixture of many colors of light. _____

Ultraviolet Rays (p. 78)

16. Electromagnetic waves with wavelengths just shorter than those of visible light are called _____.

17. Circle the letter of each sentence that is true about ultraviolet rays.

a. Too much exposure to ultraviolet rays can cause skin cancer.
b. Humans with good vision can see ultraviolet rays.
c. Ultraviolet rays cause skin cells to produce vitamin D.
d. Lamps that produce ultraviolet rays are used to kill bacteria.

X-Rays (p. 79)

18. Electromagnetic waves with frequencies higher than ultraviolet rays but lower than gamma rays are _____.

19. Circle the letter of the reason why bones show up as lighter areas on photographic plates in an X-ray machine.

a. Bones absorb X-rays and don't allow them to pass through.
b. X-rays pass right through skin and bones.
c. Bones cause the photographic plate in an X-ray machine to darken.
d. X-rays cannot pass through the skin above the photographic plates.

The Electromagnetic Spectrum ▪ *Guided Reading and Study*

Gamma Rays (p. 80)

20. The electromagnetic waves with the shortest wavelengths and the highest frequencies are called _____.

21. Why are gamma rays the most penetrating of all the electromagnetic rays?

   _____

   _____

22. Circle the letter of each sentence that is true about gamma rays.

   a. Gamma rays are produced in certain nuclear reactions.
   b. Gamma rays can be used to kill cancer cells.
   c. Gamma rays can be used to examine the body's internal structures.
   d. Gamma rays are less dangerous than X-rays.

23. Why can gamma rays from objects in space not be detected on Earth's surface?

   _____

   _____

   _____

The Electromagnetic Spectrum • *Guided Reading and Study*

Producing Visible Light (pp. 84–87)

This section describes different kinds of light bulbs.

Use Target Reading Skills

Compare and contrast the five types of light bulbs by completing the table below.

Light bulbs

Feature	Ordinary Light Bulb	Tungsten-Halogen			
Bulb material	Glass				
Hot/cool					

Introduction (p. 84)

1. Complete the table below by writing the correct term.

Kinds of Objects	
Kind of Object	**Description**
a._____ object	An object that can be seen because it reflects light
b._____ object	An object that gives off its own light

2. To view the different colors of light produced by a light bulb, you can use an instrument called a(n) _____.

Incandescent Lights (pp. 84–85)

3. A light that glows when a filament inside it gets hot is called a(n) _____.

The Electromagnetic Spectrum ▪ *Guided Reading and Study*

4. What is a tungsten-halogen light bulb?

   _____

   _____

5. Circle the letter of each sentence that is true about incandescent lights.
   a. Most of the energy produced by incandescent bulbs is given off as infrared rays.
   b. The part of an incandescent bulb that gives off light is the filament.
   c. Incandescent bulbs are very efficient in giving off light.
   d. Most ordinary incandescent light bulbs contain a small amount of gas.

6. Is the following sentence true or false? Less than ten percent of the energy of an incandescent bulb is given off as light.

   _____

7. Circle the letter of each sentence that is true about tungsten-halogen lights.
   a. Tungsten-halogen lights work like fluorescent lights.
   b. Tungsten-halogen bulbs are more efficient than ordinary light bulbs.
   c. In a tungsten-halogen light, a filament gets hot and glows.
   d. Halogen bulbs become very hot.

Other Light Sources (pp. 86–87)

8. Long, narrow glass tubes that illuminate schools and stores are _____ light bulbs.

9. Describe how a fluorescent light bulb produces visible light.

   _____

   _____

   _____

10. Circle the letter of each sentence that is true about fluorescent lights.
    a. Fluorescent lights give off most of their energy as light.
    b. Fluorescent light tubes contain a gas.
    c. Fluorescent lights emit only red light.
    d. Fluorescent lights usually don't last as long as incandescent lights.

The Electromagnetic Spectrum ▪ *Guided Reading and Study*

Producing Visible Light *(continued)*

11. Circle the letter of each sentence that is true about vapor lights.

    a. Vapor lights require very little electrical energy for a lot of light.

    b. In a vapor light, heat from gases changes a solid to a gas.

    c. Particles of sodium gas give off a greenish blue light.

    d. Vapor lights are often used for street lighting.

12. A sealed glass tube filled with neon gas that produces light is called a(n)
_____.

13. Circle the letter of each sentence that is true about neon lights.

    a. Neon lights are commonly used for bright, flashy signs.

    b. Pure neon gives out red light.

    c. Each glass neon-light tube is coated on the inside with a powder.

    d. Often, what is called a neon light contains a gas other than neon or a mixture of gases in the tube.

The Electromagnetic Spectrum · *Guided Reading and Study*

Wireless Communication (pp. 90–96)

This section describes how radio waves are used in communication, including radio, television, and cellular phones. It also describes how satellites relay information.

Use Target Reading Skills

Before you read the section, write what you know about wireless communication. As you read, continue to write in what you learn.

What You Know
I. Cellular phones don't use wires.
2.
3.

What You Learned
I.
2.
3.

Radio and Television (pp. 90–92)

1. Is the following sentence true or false? Both radio and television broadcasts are transmitted by radio waves. _____

2. What does AM stand for?

_____

Wireless Communication (continued)

3. Complete the flowchart below about the broadcast of AM radio.

The radio station transforms sound into _____ .

↓

These signals are transformed into a pattern of changes in the _____ of radio waves.

↓

Your radio picks up the radio waves and transforms them back into _____ .

4. What does FM stand for?

_____

5. How do FM signals travel?

_____

_____

6. Is the following sentence true or false? The frequencies of FM stations are lower than the frequencies of AM stations.

_____

7. Why can't FM waves be received as far away as AM waves?

_____

_____

_____

_____

8. How are television broadcasts different from radio broadcasts?

_____

_____

_____

9. What are the two main bands of television wave frequencies?

a. _____   b. _____

The Electromagnetic Spectrum ▪ *Guided Reading and Study*

Cellular Phones (p. 93)

10. Circle the letter of the type of radio waves that are transmitted and received by cellular telephones.

    a. X-rays

    b. infrared rays

    c. gamma rays

    d. microwaves

11. In a cellular telephone system, what does each cell have?

_____

12. In addition to regular phone calls, what else can you use cellular phones to do?

_____

_____

Communications Satellites (pp. 94–96)

13. Is the following sentence true or false? Communications satellites work like the receivers and transmitters of a cellular phone system.

_____

14. Circle the letter of each sentence that is true about communications satellites.

    a. It is necessary to have more than one satellite in orbit for any given purpose.

    b. Communications satellites receive sound waves from Earth and send radio waves back to Earth.

    c. Satellite phone systems can be used to communicate almost anywhere in the world.

    d. Both television networks and cable companies use communications satellites.

15. Why are television signals from satellites often scrambled?

_____

_____

16. What is the Global Positioning System?

_____

17. If you had a GPS receiver, what could you determine by receiving signals from the Global Positioning System?

_____

_____

The Electromagnetic Spectrum • *Key Terms*

Key Terms

Complete the sentences by using one of the scrambled words below.

Word Bank

ouuilmns	noothp	cancentdesin ghtsil	zieradlop
mmargoerht	oidar sevaw	andetimluli	eaoimcrwvs
uoeescntrfl ghtsli	yasr-X	iielbsv tighl	tionaidar

1. The energy that is transferred by electromagnetic waves is called electromagnetic _____.

2. Each tiny packet of light energy is called a(n) _____.

3. The electromagnetic waves with the longest wavelengths and lowest frequencies are _____.

4. The radio waves with the shortest wavelengths and the highest frequencies are _____.

5. Light that vibrates in only one direction after passing through a filter is called _____ light.

6. A picture taken with an infrared camera that shows regions of different temperatures in different colors is a(n) _____.

7. The part of the electromagnetic spectrum that you can see is called _____.

8. Electromagnetic waves with wavelengths just a little higher than ultraviolet rays are called _____.

9. An object that can be seen because it reflects light is said to be _____.

10. An object that gives off its own light is said to be _____.

11. Lights that glow when a filament inside them gets hot are called _____.

12. Lights that glow when an electric current causes ultraviolet waves to strike a coating inside a tube are called _____.

Light ▪ *Guided Reading and Study*

Light and Color (pp. 106–111)

This section explains what happens to light that strikes an object, and what determines the color of an object. It also explains how mixing colored pigments is different from mixing colored light.

Use Target Reading Skills

As you read, carefully note the definition of each key term. Also note other details in the paragraph that contains the definition. Then use all the information to write a sentence using the key term.

a. transparent material

_____

_____

b. translucent material

_____

_____

c. opaque material

_____

_____

d. primary colors

_____

_____

e. secondary colors

_____

_____

f. complementary colors

_____

_____

g. pigment

_____

_____

Light ▪ *Guided Reading and Study*

Light and Color *(continued)*

When Light Strikes an Object (p. 107)

1. What three things can happen when light strikes an object?

_____

_____

2. In which three categories can most materials be classified, based on what happens to light that strikes the material?

_____

_____

3. What happens to light that strikes a translucent material?

_____

_____

The Color of Objects (pp. 108–109)

4. The color of an opaque object is the color of the light it

_____.

5. Complete the flowchart about why you see the skin of an apple as red.

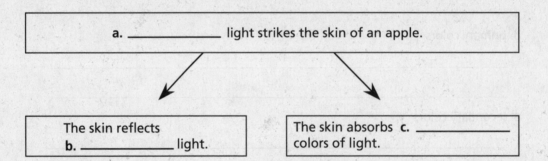

6. Is the following sentence true or false? Objects can look different in color depending on the color of light in which they are seen.

_____

7. What color does a green leaf appear to be in red light? Why?

_____

_____

Light · *Guided Reading and Study*

8. Circle the letter of the color of light that a red filter allows to pass through it.

    a. blue

    b. magenta

    c. cyan

    d. red

Combining Colors (pp. 110–111)

9. The three colors that can be used to make any other color are called _____.

10. Any two primary colors combined in equal amounts produce a(n) _____.

11. What are the three primary colors of light?

    _____

12. When combined in equal amounts, what do all three of the primary colors of light produce?

    _____

13. Complete the following "equations" by writing the secondary color the two primary colors of light produce when they are combined in equal amounts.

    a. Green + Blue _____

    b. Red + Green _____

    c. Red + Blue _____

14. Any two colors of light that combine to form white light are called _____.

15. What are pigments?

    _____

    _____

16. Complete the following "equations" by writing the secondary color the two primary colors of pigments produce.

    a. Magenta + Cyan _____

    b. Magenta + Yellow _____

    c. Cyan + Yellow _____

17. Why is the printing process called four-color printing?

    _____

    _____

Name _____ Date _____ Class _____

Reflection and Mirrors (pp. 113–118)

This section describes what happens when light rays strikes three kinds of mirrors.

Use Target Reading Skills

As you read, compare and contrast concave and convex mirrors in a Venn diagram like the one below. Write the similarities in the space where the circles overlap and the differences on the left and right sides.

Concave Mirrors   **Convex Mirrors**

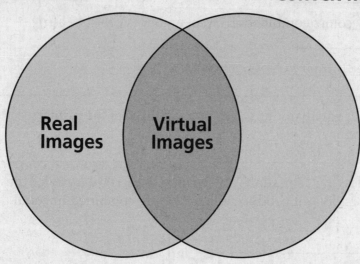

Real Images | Virtual Images

Reflection of Light Rays (p. 114)

1. Is the following sentence true or false? The reflection you see in a mirror depends on how the surface reflects light. _____

2. To show how light travels and reflects, you can represent light waves as straight lines called _____.

3. Complete the table about reflection.

Types of Reflection

Type	Surface	Nature of Reflection
a.	Smooth	b.
Diffuse	c.	Not clear

Light ▪ *Guided Reading and Study*

Plane Mirrors (p. 115)

4. What is a plane mirror?

_____

_____

_____

5. A copy of an object formed by reflected or refracted rays of light is called a(n) _____.

6. What is a virtual image?

_____

_____

_____

7. What size of image does a plane mirror produce?

_____

8. How does the image in a plane mirror differ from the object?

_____

_____

_____

Concave Mirrors (pp. 116–117)

9. A mirror with a surface that curves inward like the inside of a bowl is a(n) _____.

10. Is the following sentence true or false? The optical axis is an imaginary line that divides a mirror in half. _____

11. The point at which light rays meet is called the

_____.

12. What type of image(s) can concave mirrors form?

_____

_____

_____

13. An image formed when rays actually meet is called a(n)

_____.

Light · *Guided Reading and Study*

Reflection and Mirrors *(continued)*

Convex Mirrors (pp. 118)

14. Complete the table about kinds of mirrors.

Kinds of Mirrors			
Kind of Mirror	**Description**	**Virtual or Real Image?**	**Upright or Inverted?**
a.	Flat	**b.**	**c.**
d.	Curved inward	Virtual or real	Inverted or Upright
e.	Curved outward	**f.**	Upright

15. Why are objects in a car mirror closer than they appear?

_____

_____

_____

_____

Refraction and Lenses (pp. 119–193)

This section explains why light rays bend when they enter a medium at an angle. It also describes how images are formed when light is refracted by convex and concave lenses.

Use Target Reading Skills

Before you read, preview the red headings. In the graphic organizer below, write a what, when, where, *or* how *question for each heading. As you read, write the answers to your questions.*

Refraction and Lenses

Question	Answer
When does refraction occur?	Refraction occurs . . .

Refraction of Light (pp. 120–121)

1. When light rays enter a new medium at an angle, what does the change in speed cause the rays to do?

   _____

   _____

2. Rank the following mediums according to how fast light travels through them. Rank the fastest as *1*.

   _____ **a.** water

   _____ **b.** glass

   _____ **c.** air

3. What is a material's index of refraction?

   _____

   _____

4. Glass causes light to bend more than air does. Which material has a higher index of refraction? _____

5. Explain why a rainbow can form when light shines through tiny water droplets.

   _____

   _____

   _____

Refraction and Lenses *(continued)*

6. An image of a distant object caused by the refraction of light is called a(n) _____.

Lenses (pp. 122–123)

7. A curved piece of glass or other transparent material that is used to refract light is called a(n) _____.

8. How does a lens form an image?

_____

_____

_____

9. Label each lens as either a convex lens or a concave lens. Then draw light rays to show how light is refracted as it passes through each lens.

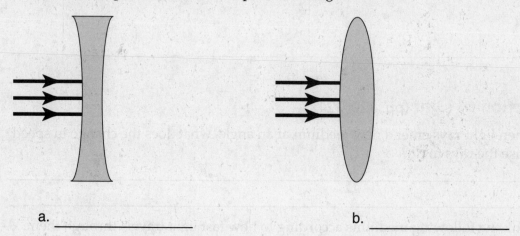

a. _____   b. _____

10. Complete the following table about lenses.

Kinds of Lenses		
Kind of Lens	**Description of Lens**	**Image Formed—Real or Virtual?**
a.	Thinner at the center than at the edges	**b.**
Convex	**c.**	Real or Virtual

Light ▪ *Guided Reading and Study*

11. What two factors determine the type of image formed by a lens?

_____

_____

12. Is the following sentence true or false? The less curved a lens is, the more it refracts light._____

13. An object's position relative to the _____ determines whether a convex lens forms a real or virtual image.

14. Why can a concave lens produce only virtual images?

_____

_____

_____

15. Is the following sentence true or false? The image formed by a concave lens is always upright and smaller than the object._____

Light • *Guided Reading and Study*

Seeing Light (pp. 125–128)

This section explains how your eyes and brain allow you to see. It also explains how lenses are used to correct vision problems.

Use Target Reading Skills

As you read about the human eye, complete the flowchart to show how you see objects. Put the steps of the process in separate boxes in the flowchart in the order in which they occur.

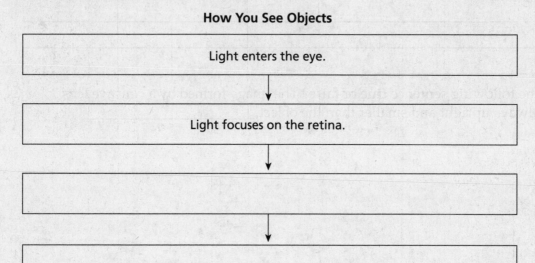

How You See Objects

Light enters the eye.

↓

Light focuses on the retina.

↓

↓

The Human Eye (pp. 126–127)

Match the part of the eye with its description.

Part of Eye

_____ 1. Cornea

_____ 2. Iris

_____ 3. Pupil

_____ 4. Lens

_____ 5. Retina

_____ 6. Optic nerve

Description

a. hole through which light enters the eye

b. transparent front surface of the eye

c. short, thick nerve through which signals travel to the brain from the eye

d. ring of muscle around the pupil

e. curved part of the eye behind the pupil, that refracts light

f. layer of cells lining the inside of the eyeball

Light · *Guided Reading and Study*

7. What part of the eye gives the eye its color?

   _____

8. The cells of the retina that respond to small amounts of light are called
   _____.

9. The cells of the retina that respond to colors are called
   _____.

10. Where does the optic nerve begin?

    _____

    _____

11. How does the brain interpret the signals from the rods and cones?

    _____

    _____

12. Label the parts of the eye on the illustration.

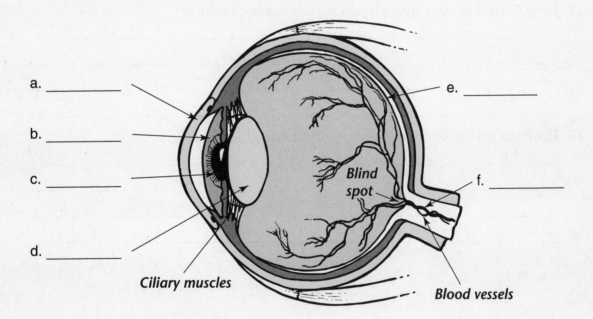

a. _____

b. _____

c. _____

d. _____

e. _____

f. _____

Blind spot

Ciliary muscles

Blood vessels

Light • *Guided Reading and Study*

Seeing Light *(continued)*

Correcting Vision (p. 128)

13. Complete the table about correcting vision.

Correcting Vision			
Vision Problem	**Shape of Eyeball**	**Vision Perception**	**Type of Correction Lens**
Nearsightedness	a.	Distant objects appear blurry	b.
c.	A little too short	d.	e.

14. How can glasses or contact lenses correct nearsightedness?

_____

_____

_____

_____

15. How can glasses or contact lenses correct farsightedness?

_____

_____

_____

_____

Light · *Guided Reading and Study*

Using Light (pp. 129–137)

This section describes how telescopes, microscopes, and cameras work. It also explains how a special kind of light, called laser light, can be used.

Use Target Reading Skills

Carefully read the definition of each key term and also read the neighboring sentences. Then write a definition of each key term in your own words.

telescope _____

_____

refracting telescope _____

_____

objective _____

_____

eyepiece _____

_____

reflecting telescope _____

_____

microscope _____

_____

camera _____

_____

laser _____

_____

hologram _____

_____

optical fiber _____

_____

total internal reflection _____

_____

Optical Instruments (pp. 130–131)

1. What are three common types of optical instruments?

_____

_____

Light · *Guided Reading and Study*

Using Light (continued)

2. An optical instrument that forms enlarged images of distant objects is called a(n) _____.

3. Complete the table about telescopes.

Types of Telescopes	
Type of Telescope	**Lenses or Mirrors?**
a.	Lenses
b.	Mirrors

4. What does the objective of a refracting telescope do?

_____

_____

5. What does the eyepiece of a refracting telescope do?

_____

_____

6. An optical instrument that forms enlarged images of tiny objects is called a(n) _____.

7. In a microscope, what is the function of the objective?

_____

_____

8. An instrument that uses one or more lenses to focus light, and film to record an image, is called a(n) _____.

9. What happens when you press the button of a camera?

_____

_____

10. How is the diaphragm of a camera like the iris of an eye?

_____

_____

_____

_____

Light · *Guided Reading and Study*

Lasers (p. 132)

11. Laser light consists of light waves that all have the same
_____, or color.

12. Is the following sentence true or false? The waves of laser light are
coherent. _____

13. What is a laser?

_____

_____

_____

Uses of Lasers (pp. 133–135)

14. Circle the letter of each choice that is a use of lasers.

    a. cutting metal
    b. scanning compact discs
    c. enlarging images of tiny objects
    d. performing surgery

15. What is a hologram?

_____

_____

_____

16. How can lasers be used in surgery?

_____

_____

_____

Optical Fibers (pp. 136–137)

17. Is the following sentence true or false? Laser beams can carry signals like
radio waves. _____

18. What are optical fibers?

_____

_____

_____

_____

Light • *Guided Reading and Study*

Using Light (continued)

19. Why can optical fibers carry a laser beam for long distances?

_____

_____

_____

20. The complete reflection of light by the inside surface of a medium is called _____.

21. Circle the letter of each sentence that is true about optical fibers.

    a. An optical fiber can carry only one telephone call at a time.

    b. Doctors use optical fibers to examine internal organs.

    c. Optical fibers make use of total internal reflection.

    d. Optical fibers have led to great improvements in computer networks.

Name _____ Date _____ Class _____

Key Terms

Answer the questions by writing the correct key terms in the blanks. Use the circled letter in each term to find the hidden key term. Then write a definition for the hidden key term.

What is a curved piece of glass or other transparent material that is used to refract light?

__ __◯__ __

What is a copy of an object formed by reflected or refracted rays of light?

__ __ __ __◯

What is an instrument that uses lenses to focus light and film to record an image?

__◯__ __ __ __

What is the transparent front surface of the eye called?

__ __◯__ __ __

What is a device that produces coherent light?

__ __◯__ __

What is an instrument that uses a combination of lenses to produce enlarged images of tiny objects?

__◯__ __ __ __ __ __ __

What are substances that are used to color other materials?

__ __◯__ __ __ __

What is a person called who can see distant objects clearly, but for whom nearby objects appear blurry?

__ __ __ __ __◯__ __ __

What is the layer of cells that line the inside of the eyeball?

__ __◯__ __ __

What is a material that reflects or absorbs all of the light that strikes it?

__ __ __ __◯__

What is the measure of how much a ray of light bends when it enters the material?

__ __◯__ __ __ __ __ __ __ __ __ __ __ __ __ __

Hidden Term: __ __ __ __ __ __ __ __ __ __ __

Definition:

_____

_____

1.

Abig white ring is placed on a hill, it acts as a lens. If the plane of the ring is to the observation is seen in the distance, it will appear as _____ of a gigantic mountain

_____ the purpose of a lens for converging the rays that is seen is to meet it will

2. What is a copy of an object captured by the reflected or bended rays called?

3. Which an image is produced as the rays are focal light and the observation is seen

4. Where is the image of the picture of the eye's vehicle

5. What is a device that produces convergent light

6. What is an image that does a combination of focus and produces certain_____ for enlarging

2. What is a device that are used for telescopes, in general?

What is an image called when all focal and object distant but it produces by the same.

What is the image of or acts in nature the centre of the eye

What is the image of optical object at of of high distances

What is the image of best pictures _____ to form bands within an object's the material